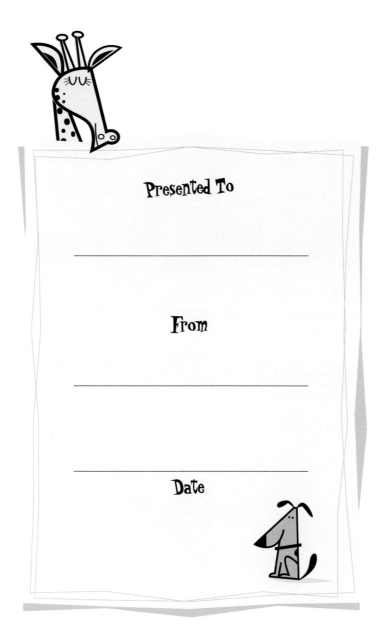

Presented To

_____

From

_____

_____

Date

I have hidden your word in my heart
that I might not sin against you.

-Psalm 119:11

THE MEMORY BIBLE

The Sure-Fire, Fun Way to Learn 52 Bible Verses

Created by Stephen Elkins

Illustrated by David Semple

INTEGRITY®
PUBLISHERS

Nashville

About the Author: S T E P H E N E L K I N S is President and owner of Wonder Workshop, the third largest independent children's music company in the world *(Billboard Magazine)*. A passionate belief in the relevancy of God's Word in everyday life has been the focus and goal of Stephen Elkins's ministry for over 15 years. The fruit of this work has resulted in over 200 Christian books, musicals, audio programs, and videos which, together, have sold over 10 million copies and earned a Grammy nomination.

T H E M E M O R Y B I B L E

Stories and songs written by Stephen Elkins.

©℗MMIII Wonder Workshop, Nashville, TN. All rights reserved. Unauthorized duplication is prohibited by law. Published by Integrity Publishers, a division of Integrity Media, Inc., 5250 Virginia Way, Suite 100, Brentwood, TN 37027.

I N T E G R I T Y P U B L I S H E R S , I N C .
HELPING PEOPLE WORLDWIDE EXPERIENCE *the* MANIFEST PRESENCE *of* GOD

Illustrated by David Semple

Cover and interior design: Russ McIntosh, The Office of Bill Chiaravalle, www.officeofbc.com

Special thanks to: The Wonder Kids Choir: Emily Elkins, Laurie Harper, Audrey Hollifield, Amy Lawrence, Lindsey McAdams, Amy McPeak, and Allie Smith.

Engineer: Randy Moore

Arrangements: John DeVries

Library of Congress Cataloging-in-Publication Data

Elkins, Stephen.
    The memory Bible : from Genesis to Revelation / created by Stephen Elkins ;
illustrations by David Semple.
        p. cm.
Includes index.
Summary : Every letter in the alphabet is represented with a Bible memory
verse, story, and song.
    ISBN 1-59145-063-2
    1.   Bible — Memorizing — Juvenile literature. [1. Bible stories. 2. Sacred
songs. 3. Alphabet.]   I. Title.
    BS617 . 7 . E45 2003
    220 . 9´505 — dc22

                                    2003011433

Printed in China

03 04 05 06 07 LEO 9 8 7 6 5 4 3 2 1

Dear Parents,

Proverbs 22:6 is truly the heart's desire of every Christian parent and guardian. We want to train up our children in the way they should go. We know they will someday face trials and temptations as even our Lord did in the wilderness. Yet, how did Jesus answer the Accuser? With scripture! He had memorized them! He was prepared for the trial. We must prepare our children, too. And *The Memory Bible* is the perfect tool to prepare them!

The Memory Bible: From Genesis to Revelation has identified 52 essential Bible verses every child should know. Genesis 1:1, John 3:16—and 50 more!—are all set to music in a contemporary style that kids will love to sing over and over again. There's just something about music that makes memorization so much easier. *The Memory Bible* is one indispensable Christian education tool to have in your home!

TRAIN UP YOUR CHILD WITH THE MEMORY BIBLE!

Stephen Elkins

A

How Awesome is the Lord Most High.

Psalm 47:2

Lots of days are very *good*. A day full of sunny, blue skies is a very good day. Other days can be *great*. A day at the beach, flying kites with your friends is a *great* day. But every now and then, you have a really awesome day.

An *awesome* day is better than good. It's even greater than great. It's the very best day of all!

9

Moses Parts the Red Sea

(Around 1446 B.C.)

Once Moses and the people of Israel had a really awesome day.

They were about to be attacked by the Egyptian army.

With the desert in front of them and the Red Sea behind them, there was no way of escape.

But God is an awesome God. He parted the Red Sea and God's people walked to safety!

What an awesome day!

11

God is more than good.

God is greater than great.

God is awesome! The Bible says there is none like Him. He is awesome because He can do all things. There is no problem too big for God. He can solve any problem, even if He has to part a sea! Got a little problem? Got a giant problem? Remember, God is better than good, greater than great. God is an awesome God!

let's sing!

How Awesome Is the Lord

Chorus
How awesome, how awesome is the Lord our God!
He is good.
How awesome, how awesome is our God!
He is an awesome God!

More than good, greater than great,
Our God is an awesome God!
He can part a sea, defeat an enemy.
Our God is an awesome God!
Oh, our God is an awesome God!

(Repeat chorus)

More than good, greater than great,
No problem too big for Him.
Oh, His mighty hand no evil can withstand.
Our God is an awesome God!
Oh, our God is an awesome God!

(Repeat chorus)

B

On my BED I remember you; I think of you through the watches of the night.

Psalm 63:6

After a busy day at school or play,

it's nice to get into your bed at night.

It's a very special time. You might fix

your pillow just right and get snuggled up in

the covers. When the lights go out, your eyes

start getting heavy. You think about all the things

you're going to do tomorrow. It's a perfect time to

whisper a little prayer.

13

David Loved to Pray

(Around 1025 B.C.)

David the shepherd boy loved to pray, too!

He spent many nights alone on the Judean hillside

watching his sheep. He watched as the moon

moved across the night sky. He heard the

sounds of wild animals in the distance.

So on his bed, before he went to sleep,

David would remember his Lord and all His promises.

He could sleep soundly knowing that God had heard his

prayers and was watching from above.

Tonight, as you lie down on your bed,

remember God's wonderful promises.

He promises to love you.

He promises to guide you.

He promises to watch over you all through the night.

Soon, instead of counting sheep, you'll find yourself

counting your blessings.

for me today!

let's sing!

On My Bed

Chorus
On my bed, I remember You.
On my bed, I remember You, Lord.
On my bed, I remember You.
I think of You through the watches of the night.
I think of You through the watches of the night.

Tonight as I lay down to sleep,
I pray my soul You'll keep tonight.
Before I drift away,
I'll think of all the blessings that have come my way.
Think of the blessings, tonight.

(Repeat chorus)

Tonight as the stars shine above,
I'll remember my Savior's love tonight.
As the moonlight shines,
I'll say a prayer 'cause I'm thankful in this heart of mine,
Thankful for the blessings, tonight.

(Repeat chorus)

God CREATED the heavens and the earth.

Genesis 1:1

It's really fun to make things

with your own hands.

With a little glue and an hour

or two, you can make almost anything.

You and Mom can make a kite out of paper and string.

You can help Dad make a birdhouse

out of wood and nails.

But do you know what God made?

17

The Creation Story

(Day 1)

God made the heavens and the earth with only His words. He spoke, and the heavens came to be. He spoke again, and the earth  was made. He used no paper or string, no wood or nails. In fact, He used nothing at all. He is so powerful and creative that He made everything with only His words!

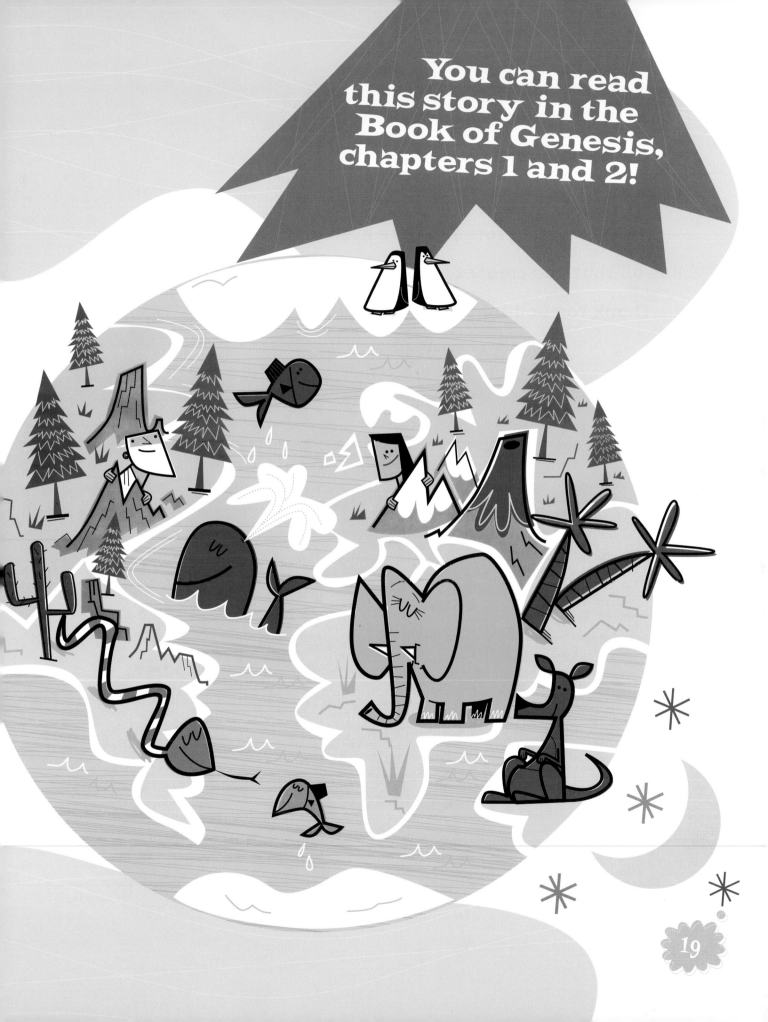

You can read this story in the Book of Genesis, chapters 1 and 2!

The Bible says that God created

the heavens and the earth.

It also says God created *you*. It says that

He knew you before you were even born.

And all that God creates is good.

Thank You God for this wonderful world

You have created.

for me today!

let's sing!

God Created

Chorus
In the beginning! Oh, in the beginning!
In the beginning,
God created the heavens and the earth.
In the beginning,
God created the heavens and the earth,
The heavens and the earth.

He is so mighty, we sing,
In the beginning! Oh, in the beginning!
With only words,
He created every living thing.
So lift your voices and sing!

(Repeat chorus)

We sing the glory of God.
In the beginning! Oh, in the beginning!
We praise His name!
Lift Him high above creation
Because He created it all!

20

D

My mouth will DECLARE your praise.

Psalm 51:15

So many different kinds of words

can come out of your mouth.

You can speak a word of kindness. You can say

"thank you." You can use words to comfort someone

in need. You can even shout an alarm: "Help!"

Your words can really make a difference

in the lives of others.

21

Solomon Was a Wise Man

(Solomon reigned from 970 to 930 B.C.)

Solomon was the wisest man ever to live.

He knew a lot of words. He used his words to write

over one thousand songs to the Lord.

He also wrote three thousand proverbs.

What a difference his words made! He used them to

declare the praise of the Lord, just like his father David.

It was Solomon who wrote:

"Saying the right word at the right time is so pleasing!"

(Proverbs 15:23 ICB) His mouth and his words declared

God's praise!

23

for me today!

How will people know that your God is a wonderful God unless you tell them? You have to show them with your actions and tell them the story of God. Sure, you believe in the Lord on the inside. But you have to start believing out loud. You can make every day a show-and-tell day. Show and tell them about God's love!

let's sing!

Declare Your Praise

My mouth will declare Your praises, Oh Lord!
My mouth will declare Your praises, Oh Lord!
I praise You for the morning sun,
Praise You for the day,
Praise You for the evening sky,
Oh Lord, I have to say...

My mouth will declare Your praises, Oh Lord!
My mouth will declare Your praises, Oh Lord!
I praise You for the moon at night,
Praise You for the stars,
Praise You Lord for all You've done,
Praise You for who You are!

E:

Let EVERYTHING that has breath praise the LORD.

Psalm 150:6

THINKIN' **2day**

You have breath, right?

What do you use it for? Dogs can use their breath to bark. Cats can use their breath to meow. Birds can sing, and lions can roar. But only people can use their breath to speak and sing. You can use words to express your thoughts. But most of all, you should use your breath to praise the Lord!

25

Noah and the Flood

(Around 2344 B.C.)

Noah once breathed in

the funny smell of thousands of animals

all packed into one boat. But he spoke out words of

praise to God, because he loved the Lord! God told

Noah to build an ark and gather all the animals together,

two  of every kind. Noah obeyed.

The flood waters came and destroyed all the evil people.

But Noah and his family were saved!

If you have breath, you are alive. And if you are alive, you should give thanks to the Lord for all He has done. You should praise Him, for life is the most important gift God has given to you. Share the gift. Tell others about God's love. And as long as you have breath, praise the Lord.

Let Everything That Has Breath

Let everything, everything that has breath,
Let everything, everything that has breath,
Praise the Lord, praise the Lord I say!
Can you hear me today?
Come on every girl and boy,
Make a mighty noise and praise the Lord!

Let everything, everything that has breath,
Let everything, everything that has breath,
Praise the Lord, praise the Lord with me!
'Til all the world can see,
He is a great and mighty God.
So where e'er your feet may trod, praise the Lord!

F

MY MEMORY **verse**

A FRIEND loves at all times.
Proverbs 17:17

THINKIN' **2day**

There's nothing better than having a good friend you can count on—someone who's always there in good times and bad. Someone you can talk to and someone who'll listen.  That's the kind of friend you should try to be to others. "Fair-weather" friends seem to disappear when things get tough. But a real friend is always  there to give a smile, to listen, and to help!

29

Jonathan and David Were Friends

(Around 1010 B.C.)

Jonathan and David were best friends. Jonathan's father was the king of Israel, so David and Jonathan stayed in the palace.

They enjoyed being together. They respected each other. Jonathan gave David his robe and tunic, even his sword and his bow! When bad times came, Jonathan showed David that he was a true friend.

31

Real friendship is based on love and a giving spirit. Jonathan had a giving spirit. You, too, can show your friendship by giving of your time, your abilities, and even sharing your things to help others. A friend loves at all times: the good times, the bad times . . . any time. And that's what true friendship is all about!

for me today!

let's sing!

A Friend Loves at All Times!

Oh, a friend loves at all times!
Oh, a friend loves at all times!
Morning, noon, or night,
A friend is a delight,
For a friend loves at all times!

Oh, a friend loves at all times!
Oh, a friend loves at all times!
When evening shadows fall,
A friend will come to call,
For a friend loves at all times!

Oh, a friend loves at all times!
Oh, a friend loves at all times!
When stars do shine above,
A friend will speak in love,
For a friend loves at all times!

A Gentle answer turns away wrath.

Proverbs 15:1

People can have different views on the same subject. Some like the rain; some do not. Some like it cold; some like it hot. Sometimes differences can cause tempers to flare. If you're not careful, your disagreement can turn into an argument. In those times, you should be very careful with your words. It is more difficult to settle a disagreement when someone is angry.

33

Jesus Gave a Gentle Answer

(Around A.D. 29)

The religious leaders and teachers brought a woman to Jesus. She had broken the law. These leaders had angry hearts. They thought she should be killed with stones.

They asked Jesus if he thought they were doing the right thing. But Jesus answered, "If any one of you is without sin, let him be the first to throw a stone." (John 8:7) Suddenly, it got very quiet. They all walked away ashamed. Jesus' soft answer turned them away and saved the young woman.

You can read this story in John, chapter 8!

35

Sometimes, you may have disagreements with others. Even friends and family may get very angry. If this happens, it is always best to do what Jesus did. He spoke a gentle answer. Shouting unkind words at each other won't help you settle your argument. Be like Jesus. Speak a gentle word.

for me today!

let's sing!

A Gentle Answer

Chorus
A gentle answer turns away the wrath
Of those who come your way. I say,
A gentle answer calms the voice,
Stills the heart; it's heaven's choice.

A gentle word, a voice so kind
Can move a heart, change a mind.
A gentle word, a voice of love
Calms a spirit with joy because

(Repeat chorus)

A gentle voice, a word of peace,
Can calm the soul, make wars cease.
A gentle voice, a glad refrain
Is like a medicine that soothes the pain.

(Repeat chorus)

H

Love the LORD your God with all your HEART and with all your soul and with all your strength.

Deuteronomy 6:5

Twenty anxious girls sat down on the gym floor. Coach Maxwell came into the room and spoke. "If you are going to play basketball for the Thunder Cats, I will be here every evening, Monday through Friday, from 4:00 to 7:00. You will need to be here every day for practice." Emily's hand slowly went up into the air. "I have piano lessons on Tuesdays at 5:00. May I be excused for that?" The coach answered, "Absolutely not!" Emily loved playing the piano more than she loved basketball. She would not be able to try out for basketball. She could not give her all to the team.

The Rich, Young Ruler

(Around A.D. 30)

A rich, young man once came to Jesus.

He asked what he must do to have eternal life.

Jesus said that he must keep *all* the commandments.

The young man said that he had kept all the commandments. Then Jesus said that he should sell *all* he owned and give to the poor.

But the young man could not do this because he loved the things he owned more than he loved the Lord.

He didn't love God with *all* of his heart.

God wants you to love Him with your whole heart. If you are half-hearted in your love for Him, you may be saving the other half for the things of this world. Nothing in this world should keep you from heaven. Today, love God with *all* your heart and see the difference!

for me today!

let's sing!

With All Your Heart

God wants us to really love Him,
Love Him with all our hearts,
Night or day, work or play.
If you travel far away,
It doesn't matter wherever you are.
You know that God wants us to really love Him,
Love Him with all our hearts.
The Bible says,
Love the Lord with all your heart
And with all your soul
And with all your strength.

God wants us to really love Him,
Love Him with all our hearts.
Stay awhile; pray awhile.
Tell Him 'bout your day awhile,
It doesn't matter wherever you are,
You know that God wants us to really love Him,
Love Him with all our hearts.
The Bible says,
Love the Lord with all your heart
And with all your soul
And with all your strength.

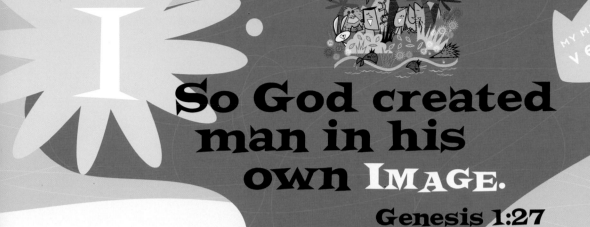

So God created man in his own IMAGE.

Genesis 1:27

Do you remember a time when the circus came to town? Did you go into the house of mirrors? You probably couldn't believe how funny it made you look! In one mirror, you looked short and fat.

In another, you appeared to be tall and skinny. Your image would change with every mirror. It would be easy to forget what you really looked like!

Adam and Eve

(Day 6)

God made human beings in His own image.

Adam and Eve were perfect in every way. God put them in the Garden of Eden where they would have everything they needed. God blessed them and said,

"Have many children and grow in number. Fill the earth and be its master . . . Rule over every living thing that moves on the earth." (Genesis 1:28 ICB)

Then God said it was very good!

You can read the whole story in Genesis, chapter 1!

43

Some people have forgotten for me today! what they are supposed to look like on the inside. They were created in the image of God. Yet because of their sinful habits, it's hard to see God in them.

God is joyful and loving. You should be, too! God is honest and trustworthy. You should be, too! God is faithful and just. Yes—you should be, too! This world can bend your image like a house of mirrors. But don't forget, you were made in the image of God!

In His Own Image

Chorus
God created, so God created,
God created, so God created,
God created man in His own image, oh, yeah!

We know God made the heavens.
We know God made the earth.
We know God made the oceans.
He made the beautiful surf.
We know God made a woman.
We know God made a man.
We know He created them in His image.
Please understand.

(Repeat chorus)

We know God made the mountains.
We know God made the seas.
We know God made the deserts.
He made the beautiful trees.
We know God made a woman.
We know God made a man.
We know He created them in His image.
Please understand.

(Repeat chorus)

J

"The JOY of the LORD is your strength."

Nehemiah 8:10

THINKIN'
2day

Robert was a member of the Cub Scouts.

There was nothing he wanted more than to earn his

Arrow of Light award! So when other kids were playing

video games or watching cartoons,

Robert worked hard to reach his goal.

He knew the sacrifice would be worth it when they

presented the badge to him at the Pack meeting.

The thought of the joy of that

moment kept him going!

45

Paul Lives a Godly Life

(Around A.D. 59-61)

Paul knew how difficult it was to work toward a great reward. When he chose to live a Godly life, people made fun of him, and he was even put in jail! But Paul kept going, knowing the reward in the end would be worth it all. And at the end of his struggles, he looked back and said, "I have fought the good fight, I have finished the race, I have kept the faith. Now there is in store for me the crown of righteousness, which the Lord . . . will award to me on that day." (2 Timothy 4:7–8)

When you have a tough job to do,

just thinking about the reward to come

is enough to keep you going!

In your Christian journey, you may face

many trials. But the joy of knowing that God's

servants are bound for heaven will help you through the day,

the year, even the rest of your life.

Yes, the joy of the Lord is your strength to reach the finish line!

for me today!

let's sing!

The Joy of the Lord

Chorus
I've got the joy, joy, joy down in my heart!
I've got the joy, joy, joy down in my heart
'Cause the joy of the Lord is my strength!
Yes, indeed!
The joy of the Lord is my strength!
Say it again!
The joy of the Lord is my strength!
Yes, indeed!
The joy of the Lord is my strength!

When trouble comes my way, Lord,
All I have to say, Lord,
The joy of the Lord is my strength
'Cause I know my Lord is there
To fight my battles anywhere, oh yeah!

(Repeat chorus)

When sadness fills my day, Lord,
Bad news comes my way, Lord,
The joy of the Lord is my strength!
'Cause I know my Lord is there
To fight my battles anywhere, oh yeah!

(Repeat chorus)

K

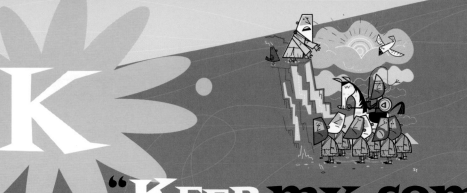

"KEEP my commands and you will live."

Proverbs 4:4

THINKIN'
2day

The rain was pouring down.

The wipers could barely clear the windshield.

Thunder crashed and lightning filled the sky.

It was only a few more miles to the bridge.

Suddenly, Juan saw a very bright light up ahead.

A policeman with a flare was standing in the downpour.

"The bridge is out!" he shouted. "Go back!"

Juan's dad thanked the policeman.

His warning had saved their lives.

49

Jeremiah Reminds Israel

(Around 587 B.C.)

The prophet Jeremiah warned Israel to never ignore God's warnings. The nation of Israel had served and obeyed God for many years. But as time passed, the people forgot about God's commands. They began to sin more and more. Soon, an enemy of Israel came and made them their slaves. Jeremiah wept for the nation of Israel. But he reminded them that even though they had forgotten God,

God had not forgotten them.

God's commandments show you the
way and serve as a warning.
They are like light in a very dark world.
They show you the right way to live your life.
They are also a warning, telling you, "There's danger ahead!
Don't go that way!" Every day you must choose to obey or
ignore God's commands. If you obey His commands,
you will live an exciting life!

let's
sing!

Keep My Commands

Chorus
Keep My commandments and you will live.
Keep My commandments and you will live.
If you keep My commandments,
You will live.
If you keep My commandments,
You will live; you will live.

God's Word is like a flare in the darkest night,
Showing us the way.
God's Word is like a flare shining forth its light,
Helping us to see where we ought to be.

(Repeat chorus)

God's word is wonderful, keeping us from harm,
Showing us the way.
God's word is wonderful; it sounds a big alarm,
When sin I do see there in front of me.

(Repeat chorus)

Your word is a LAMP to my feet and a light for my path.

Psalm 119:105

One summer, Lindsay visited her grandfather's farm. After dinner each night, she and Granddad would walk down a small path to the barn to check on the horses.  Since the path had no lights, Granddad would carry a lantern to light the way.

 Granddad knew the way so well, Lindsay would stay close to him and walk in the light.

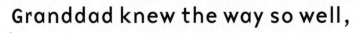

Paul on the Damascus Road

(Around A.D. 35)

The missionary Paul wasn't always a believer in Jesus Christ. In fact, before he became a Christian, his name was Saul. Saul spent his days looking for Christians so he could put  them into prison. One day as he neared Damascus, a bright light flashed around him.

Then he heard a voice saying, "Why do you persecute Me?" (Acts 9:4) Saul was afraid and asked, "Who are You?" The voice answered, "I am Jesus." (Acts 9:5–6) Saul was blinded by the bright light. But three days later, he could see once again.

When Saul became a Christian, his name was changed to Paul. He taught many people about Jesus.

55

God's Word is like a lamp. It allows you to see clearly the things ahead. Without a lamp, you might stumble and fall. You may wonder what tomorrow might bring. But don't worry, God has that under control. Just stay close to your Father by praying, obeying, and studying the Bible. And step into God's light!

for me today!

let's sing!

Your Word Is a Lamp

Chorus
Your word is a lamp to my feet
And a light for my path.
Wherever I am going,
Your word is a lamp to my feet
And a light for my path,
Wherever I go.

Just like a candle in the darkness,
You show me the way to go.
Just like a candle in the darkness,
You brighten my life, I know.

(Repeat chorus)

Just like a candle in the darkness,
I can see all around me there.
Just like a candle in the darkness,
Your light's shining everywhere.

(Repeat chorus)

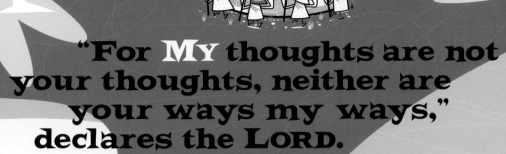

"For **My** thoughts are not your thoughts, neither are your ways my ways," declares the **Lord**.

Isaiah 55:8

"Hiccup!" *What do I have to do to make these things go away?* Michael wondered. He walked over to Dad, opened his mouth to speak, and—"Hiccup!" With a grin, Dad instructed, "Hold your breath and swallow ten times." Michael gave him a funny look, but unable to question him—"Hiccup!"—Michael tried it. And what do you know?

The hiccups went away!

Joshua and the Battle of Jericho

(Around 1400 B.C.)

Joshua's army crossed the Jordan River into the Promised Land. There, they would battle the Canaanites at Jericho. But the Lord told Joshua to do a very strange thing. To win the battle, the Lord told him to march around the walls of Jericho once a day for six days. Then, on the seventh day, march again, sound the trumpets, and shout! Even though it sounded strange, Joshua obeyed the Lord. The walls of Jericho fell exactly like the Lord said they would!

What a strange way to win a battle! Joshua's army didn't use their strength. They didn't use their weapons. They didn't need to.

They simply obeyed God's command. God's ways are not your ways. Sometimes He does things a little differently than you might do them. But no matter what today may bring, you must be of good courage like Joshua. And you must trust your heavenly Father.

He always knows the best way!

My Thoughts Are Not Your Thoughts

Chorus
"For My thoughts are not your thoughts,
Neither are your ways My ways,"
Declares the Lord to all who will believe.
"For My thoughts are not your thoughts,
Neither are My ways, your ways,"
Declares the Lord to all who will believe.

Do you believe in the Lord who is almighty?
Yes, we do!
Have courage and wait upon the Lord.
Do you believe in the Lord who is almighty?
Alrighty then!
Have courage, wait upon the Lord!

(Repeat chorus)

Do you believe in the Lord who's always listening?
Yes, we do!
Have courage and call upon the Lord.
Do you believe in the Lord who's always listening?
I'm insisting!
Have courage, wait upon the Lord!

(Repeat chorus)

N

MY MEMORY **verse**

The **NAME** of the **LORD** is a strong tower; the righteous run to it and are safe.

Proverbs 18:10

THINKIN' 2day

Smoke poured from the windows of the grocery store.  A crowd soon gathered, making it difficult to pass through the street. Shoppers, reporters, and concerned onlookers all pushed against one another to watch the scene unfold.

Suddenly, the crowd parted to allow one man to walk through. He didn't say a word. He didn't have to.

It read "Fire Department" across his badge, and the crowd knew he was there to help.

Esther Saved Her People

(Around 480 B.C.)

Esther knew there was great power in the name of the Lord. She knew it could demand authority even with kings! Esther, a Jew, was the Queen of Persia. She discovered an evil plot by a man named Haman. He was planning to kill all of the Jews.

Esther spoke to her cousin, Mordecai. Mordecai called upon the name of the Lord and asked Him to help his people. Esther then asked King Xerxes to help her. Her request was granted. The name of the Lord is mighty. The Lord will help His people when they call upon Him.

You can read the whole story in the Book of Esther!

The name of the Lord affords you a great privilege. His name can move crowds. It can move kings. His name has great authority when you call upon God.

Situations can sometimes be very frightening, and you can be tempted to give in to pressure.

But don't let the situation change your faith. Let your faith change the situation. Because the name of the Lord is like a strong tower, you'll be safe with Him!

for me today!

let's sing!

The Name of the Lord

Chorus
The name of the Lord is a strong tower;
The righteous run to it and are safe.
The name of the Lord is a strong tower;
The righteous run to it and are safe.
The righteous run to it and are safe.

In the Old Testament,
There is a name I love to sing.
In the Old Testament,
There is a name; life it brings.
Yahweh,
Great and mighty You are.
Yahweh, I give You my life.
Come into my heart.

(Repeat chorus)

In the New Testament,
There is a name I love to sing.
In the New Testament,
There is a name joy it brings.
Jesus,
Great and mighty You are.
Jesus, I give You my life.
Come into my heart.

(Repeat chorus)

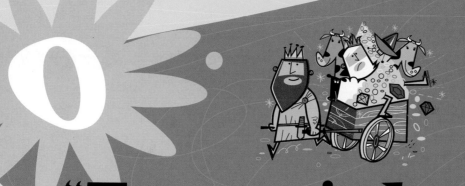

O

"To OBEY is better than sacrifice."
1 Samuel 15:22

THINKIN' 2day

There are probably a lot of UFO Christians around your church. A missionary once spoke about UFOs. She encouraged everyone to be of Unwavering faith, to Fear the Lord, and to be Obedient. Wouldn't it be awesome if every church was filled with UFOs? (But, watch out. People *might* think you're a little weird if you say you've seen a UFO . . .)

King Saul Disobeyed God

(Around 1015 B.C.)

Bible Story

King Saul was not a UFO believer. He disobeyed the Lord. The Lord told Saul to destroy an evil enemy. Instead, Saul spared the evil king and took all the king's treasures for himself. Samuel asked Saul why he had disobeyed. Saul said that he had obeyed *most* of what God told him, and he would give God a portion of the treasures. Samuel said, "To obey is better than sacrifice." (1 Samuel 15:22) Saul was sorry for disobeying God.

You can read the whole story in 1 Samuel, chapter 15!

for me today!

More than your time, more than your money, God wants your obedience. That is most important to Him. It is not enough to obey only a *part* of what He asks. But if you strive to obey Him *completely*, you will make God happy. God's commands are wise. Obey cheerfully!

let's sing!

To Obey Is Better

To obey is better than sacrifice,
So obey the Lord, dear children.

(Repeat in a round 5 times)

"O" It's the Only way to go.
"B" Be certain it's true.
"E" Everybody should obey.
"Y" You and I should, too.

Obey!

P

"For I know the PLANS I have for you, declares the LORD."

Jeremiah 29:11

2day

It was Maria's birthday, and no one remembered. *No cake, no candles, no party . . . how could they forget?* she wondered. Mom walked in and said, "I don't feel like cooking tonight. Let's just go to Pizza Palace to eat." When they arrived, Dad told Maria, "Go sit at that table while I order." Maria sat down and found a letter on the table with her name on it. The note inside read, "Go to the Play Room." When Maria walked into the Play Room, "Surprise!" came the shouts of all her friends. "We've been planning this day for weeks!" Mom told her. "Did you really think we had forgotten your birthday?"

Jeremiah Gives Hope

(Around 627 B.C.)

Jeremiah once sent a very special letter to the priests and prophets of Israel who were in captivity. It was a letter from God. The Jews thought that God had forgotten about them. But Jeremiah's letter from God promised that He had not forgotten them, that He had great plans for them, and He would soon set them free. Hearing God's plan brought hope to the people.

Sometimes when you're most discouraged,
God is planning something wonderful for you.
God knows the needs in your life, and
He never forgets a single prayer. At just
the time you need it most —surprise!— God
steps in with many surprises.

He has great plans for your life!

for me today!

let's sing!

I Know the Plans I Have for You

Chorus
I know the plans I have for you,
Declares the Lord.
I know the plans I have for you,
Declares the Lord.

I will prosper you in all you do.
I will be there to guide you.
I will be a friend until the end.
You can depend on Me.

(Repeat chorus)

I will guard your way and every day.
I'll be there beside you.
I will hear your prayer; I'm always there.
You can count on Me.

(Repeat chorus)

"He will QUIET you with his love."
Zephaniah 3:17

No one thought that little baby would *ever* stop crying! She started with a whimper that turned into a whine that grew into a cry that exploded into a WAIL!

Everyone in the restaurant turned to look. *What did the baby need?* A frantic mother came running back to the table.  The mom took her baby in her arms and gave her a long-awaited bottle. That's all the baby needed. She was really quiet after that!

Jesus Calms the Storm

(Around A.D. 28)

Bible Story

One day, the disciples needed to calm down. As they were sailing across a lake, Jesus went to sleep in the back of the boat. And as he slept, a terrible storm came upon them. The waves were so high! The disciples were afraid. They woke Jesus and shouted, "Teacher, don't You care if we drown?" (Mark 4:38) Jesus awoke.

Seeing they were afraid, He said to the sea, "Quiet! Be still!" (Mark 4:39) And the storm stopped!

It was amazing! Even the wind and waves obey Jesus!

You can read
this story
in Mark 4:35-41!

75

Sometimes there is a storm brewing inside of you. Something is wrong.

for me today!

Maybe you have a hard decision to make. Maybe your feelings have been hurt.

Maybe you've done something bad. But God can bring peace to a troubled heart. Jesus can turn all your hurts into hopes. If He can calm a wild sea, He can surely calm you! Today, ask Jesus to calm the storms in your life.

let's sing!

He Will Quiet You

Chorus
He will quiet you!
He will quiet you!
He will quiet you with His love, His love, oh!
He will quiet you!
He will quiet you!
He will quiet you with His love, His love!
Oh, God!

When the storm is raging inside your heart,
He can calm you; He can calm you.
When the world around you is falling apart,
He can calm the storm!

(Repeat chorus)

When you're hurt and lonely 'n ready to fall,
He can calm you; He can calm you.
When your heart is troubled, no one to call,
He can calm the storm.

R

REMEMBER your Creator in the days of your youth.

Ecclesiastes 12:1

THINKIN' 2day

Erin can be so forgetful sometimes. The other day, she had a flat tire on her bicycle. No problem! She knew how to fix it. She was almost finished when Mom called for lunch. After lunch, she went back down to the garage and hopped on her bike. Off she went, but suddenly, the front wheel started wobbling. It came completely off the bicycle! She had forgotten something very important: she had forgotten to tighten the nuts that hold the tire in place!

Josiah, the Young King

(Around 622 B.C.)

Josiah's father was the king of Israel.

But he had forgotten something very important.

He had forgotten about the Lord and

worshiped idols instead. Josiah became king

when he was only eight years old. He destroyed the

idols and sent workers to repair the temple of the Lord.

Then the Book of the Law was found, covered with

dust. The book was read to the young king.

Upon hearing the Word, he knew his people

had sinned. Josiah asked God for forgiveness.

Josiah promised 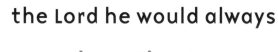 the Lord he would always

remember Him.

Memory is really a cool thing. It helps you to make the right choices. It helps you to live your life with fewer difficulties. If you remember God's Word, you can act upon it and live a good life. If you forget about God, it can bring terrible trouble. In all that you do, remember the Lord, your Creator, and His commands.

Don't forget to remember the Creator this week!

for me today!

let's sing!

Remember Your Creator

Remember your Creator in the days of your youth!
Remember your Creator in the days of your youth!
Remember your Creator in the days of your youth,
And you will live a happy life! Amen!
Don't forget, don't forget,
To remember the Lord and His promises!
Don't forget, don't forget,
To remember the Lord and His promises!

(Repeat)

The LORD is my SHEPHERD, I shall not be in want.

Psalm 23:1

THINKIN' 2day

It was almost midnight when the group reached the river. They unloaded in a clearing next to the Appalachian Trail. The guide, Mr. Evans, said they would set up camp there. In the morning, they would begin their adventure through Newfoundland Gap. Mr. Evans had been there before. He knew the way. He had the compass and map. He would lead them. And like sheep, they would gladly follow!

David, the Shepherd Boy

(Around 1025 B.C.)

David learned how to be a shepherd when he was a small boy. He knew that sheep weren't very smart. In fact, they were pretty goofy animals. They needed to be led or they would go the wrong way. They needed to be fed because they couldn't find a good pasture by themselves. They needed a protector who cared about them, because they couldn't defend themselves. David learned that shepherds lead the sheep, feed the sheep, and take care of the sheep.

You can read
this story in
1 Samuel 17:34-37!

He knows your needs. And if you choose to follow Him, He will lead you.

He will lead you in paths of righteousness.

A path is not a freeway. So you may not see many others walking the same way you are.

But He's the Good Shepherd.

He knows what you need and the way that is best for you!

for me today!

let's sing!

The Lord Is My Shepherd

Chorus
The Lord is, the Lord is my shepherd.
The Lord is, the Lord is my shepherd.
The Lord is, the Lord is my shepherd.
How about you?
Yes He is!

The Lord is like a shepherd; He knows what to do.
The Lord is like a shepherd; He'll walk with you.
The Lord is like a shepherd; He knows what to do.
When His little lambs are tired, He'll help them through!
When His little lambs are tired, He'll help them through!

The Lord is like a shepherd; He guards my way.
The Lord is like a shepherd, watching night and day.
The Lord is like a shepherd; He guides my way,
Keeping all the enemies far, far away,
Keeping all the enemies far, far away.

Give THANKS to the LORD, for he is good.

Psalm 136:1

The girls' gymnastics team was traveling in a small van to a competition. It was beginning to snow, when suddenly, the engine began to sputter. To everyone's horror, the van just stopped. There they sat, broken down in the snow. A few minutes later, a truck driver pulled in behind the van. "Having trouble?" he asked. Then the man opened the hood, made some adjustments, and—*vrooom!*—the engine started. In all of the excitement, the team forgot to say "thank you"—all except Cindy. She ran back to the man's truck and said, "Thanks, Mister!" He smiled as he drove away.

The Ten Lepers

(Around A.D. 30)

Once Jesus was on His way to Jerusalem. He met ten men who had leprosy. They cried out, "Jesus, Master, have pity on us!" (Luke 17:13) Jesus told them to go and show themselves to the priest. As they went, they were healed! But only one of the ten men came back to thank Jesus for what He had done.

Jesus asked, "Were not all ten cleansed? Where are the other nine?" (Luke 17:17) Jesus blessed the one who said "thank you."

You can read this story in Luke 17:11-19!

87

From the time you were very small, you've probably been taught to say "thank you." But do you remember to thank the most important One of all? Let God know every day how thankful you are.

Thank Him for His protection. Thank Him for the love He has shown to you. Thank Him for His goodness to you and your family. Offer a prayer of thanksgiving this very minute.

He is a good God!

for me today!

let's sing!

O, Give Thanks

Chorus
O, give thanks to the Lord!
O, give thanks for He is good!
O, give thanks to the Lord!
O, give thanks for He is good!
Lift up your praises; let all the children say,
Lift up your praises to the Lord today!
O, give thanks to the Lord!
O, give thanks for He is good!

Thank Him, thank Him, thank Him for the blue sky.
Thank Him for eyes to see the world.
Thank Him, thank Him, all you children.
Thank Him, every boy and girl!

(Repeat chorus)

Thank Him, thank Him, thank Him for Jesus.
Thank Him for all He's done for you.
Thank Him, thank Him, all you children.
Thank Him, it's what we all should do!

(Repeat chorus)

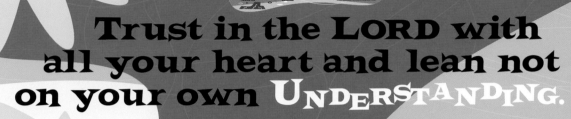

MY MEMORY verse

Trust in the LORD with all your heart and lean not on your own UNDERSTANDING.

Proverbs 3:5

THINKIN' 2day

Dylan buckled his seat belt and looked out the window. It was the biggest engine he'd ever seen. This was his first airplane ride, and he was a little nervous. "How can this thing fly? Maybe we should get off," he told his mom. She leaned out and whispered to the passing flight attendant. The attendant smiled at Dylan and said, "Come with me." He walked with the attendant to the front of the plane. The pilot turned and said, "Welcome aboard! What can I do for you, young man?" Dylan spoke up, "How does the plane fly?" The pilot answered, "It's a little hard to understand, but trust me. I'll get you there safely. Just leave it to me." That's all Dylan needed to hear!

Mary Trusts God

(Around 6 B.C.)

Mary was confused. Nothing the angel had said to her made sense. She was engaged to a man named Joseph, but they weren't married yet. How could she be having a baby? She didn't understand. The angel said to her, "Do not be afraid, Mary, you have found favor with God. You will be with child and give birth to a Son, and you are to give Him the name Jesus." (Luke 1: 30–31) That's all Mary needed to hear. She answered, "I am the Lord's servant. . . May it be to me as you have said." (Luke 1:38)

You can read
the whole story
in Luke 1:26-38!

91

The Lord is like a pilot.

And many times He simply says,

"Trust Me. This will be very hard to

understand, but I plan to get you there safely.

Just leave it to Me." Can you trust Him?

Because Mary trusted Him, a Savior was born who

would later die to free the world from sin. You can trust Him,

too! Even when you do not understand, trust Him—not your

feelings. Lean on Him—not your understanding.

And know that *He* is in control—not you. That's real trust!

Lean Not on Your Own Understanding

Chorus
Trust in the Lord with all your heart.
Trust in the Lord with all your heart.
Trust in the Lord with all your heart,
And lean not on your own understanding.
Trust in the Lord with all your heart.
Trust in the Lord with all your heart.
Trust in the Lord with all your heart, my friend.

The Lord is like a pilot,
And many times He says,
"Trust in Me; trust in Me."
The Lord is like a pilot,
In times of greatest need,
"Trust in Me; trust in Me."

(Repeat chorus)

The Lord will be my captain.
Him I will obey.
Trust in Him; trust in Him.
The Lord will be my captain.
He'll lead me all the way.
Trust in Him; trust in Him.

(Repeat chorus)

V

In the morning, O LORD, you hear my VOICE.

Psalm 5:3

THINKIN'
2day

Katy had just woken up from the scariest nightmare! She sat straight up in her bed and looked around in the darkness. "Mom?" she called in a meek voice. In seconds, Mom stood at her doorway, turned on the light, and came to Katy's side to comfort her. "I'm here. It's all right," she whispered. Katy's mom was right there when Katy called, even in the wee hours of the morning.

93

Joshua Calls on God

(Around 1400 B.C.)

Bible Story

Joshua knew he could call on God at any time. When great forces stood against Joshua and his army, he called out to God for help. God answered his call. He told Joshua, "Do not be afraid of them; I have given them into your hand." (Joshua 10:8) God confused the enemy, and Joshua and his men marched in and took them by surprise. With the power of God behind him, Joshua and his army defeated the mighty forces against them.

You can read
the whole story
in Joshua, chapter 10!

Many wake up each morning and never even think about the Lord. They go about their day with good health and blessings, never thinking of the One who has given it all to them. Let the Lord hear your voice. Let Him know you're thankful for all He's done in your life. When you get up and begin a new day, let God hear your voice, and take time to listen to His.

for me today!

let's sing!

You Hear My Voice

In the morning, Lord, You hear my voice.
In the morning, Lord, You hear me call.
In the morning, Lord, You hear my voice,
Praising who You are, saying,

Chorus
Holy, holy You are!
Worthy, worthy You are!
Honor we give to Your name!
Hear us Lord, our glad refrain!
Hear us Lord, our glad refrain!

At noontime, Lord, You hear my voice.
At noontime, Lord, You hear me call.
At noontime, Lord, You hear my voice,
Praising who You are, saying,

(Repeat chorus)

At bedtime, Lord, You hear my voice.
At bedtime, Lord, You hear me call.
At bedtime, Lord, You hear my voice,
Praising who You are, saying. . .

(Repeat chorus)

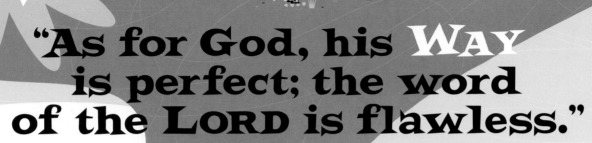

"As for God, his WAY is perfect; the word of the LORD is flawless."

2 Samuel 22:31

THINKIN'
2day

Ben and his dad just stared at the map, confused.

Some roads followed along the shore.

Some went to the shore and circled back into

the mainland. But none went across to the tiny island.

How could they get there? "Nobody gets to the island

except by the ferry," the man at the gas station

told them. So Ben and his dad bought

their tickets for the ten o'clock ferry, and off they went.

Sometimes, there's only one way to get there!

Jesus Is the Way

(Around A.D. 30)

Jesus once told His disciples that He was going to go and prepare a place for them. He said He would return and take them to where He was. He told them, "You know the way to the place where I am going." (John 14:4) Thomas asked, "Lord, we don't know where you're going, so how can we know the way?" Jesus answered, "I am the way and the truth and the life. No one comes to the Father except through Me." (John 14:5–6)

God's way isn't always the easy way, but it's the way to peace. God's way isn't always the short way, but it's the way home. God's way isn't always the fast way, but it is the right way. Jesus said, "I am the way." The only way! If you want to know and love God, you need to follow Jesus.

let's sing!

His Way Is Perfect

Lots of ways to go,
Lots of ways you know.
As for God, His way is perfect.
Many roads to take,
Some a big mistake.
As for God, His way is perfect.
Oh, He's waiting for you,
Waiting to show His way!
Oh, He's waiting for you,
So walk with Him today!

Chorus
As for God, His way is perfect.
As for God, His way is true.
The Word of the Lord is flawless,
So let's walk with Him, please do!

Jesus is the way
For the world today.
As for God, His way is perfect.
Detour up ahead!
Don't wanna be misled.
As for God, His way is perfect.
Oh, He's waiting for you,
Waiting to show His way!
Oh, He's waiting for you,
So walk with Him today!

(Repeat chorus)

X

Glorify the LORD with me; let us eXALT his name together.

Psalm 34:3

The two brothers were as different as night and day.

But they had one thing in common. They both wanted to make a Christmas gift for their mom. So Jason, the artistic one, decided to paint a picture.

Chad, the practical one, decided to make a coupon book filled with chores he would do for his mother. They both loved their mother very much.

They just had different ways of expressing it. Mom loved both gifts because she knew her sons were using their own talents to give her a

gift from their hearts.

Mary and Martha

Mary and Martha were sisters.

They both loved the Lord very much. But they chose

different ways to show it. Martha served the Lord with

her great service. Mary simply worshiped Him.

One day, Jesus came to their home. Martha

warmly welcomed Jesus and started preparing food.

But Mary sat at Jesus' feet and worshiped Him.

Martha felt like she was doing all the work. She said,

"Lord, . . . Tell her to help me!" (Luke 10:40) Jesus

told Martha that Mary had her own way of worshipping.

Both ways were good! Mary and Martha each used their

own way to exalt the Lord.

You can read this story in Luke 10:38-42!

103

People are very different in how they express their love for the Lord.

Some glorify God with their service. They may help collect food for the hungry or empty the trash at church. Some sing; some play games with the children. In whatever you do, glorify the Lord, and proclaim His glory throughout the whole earth!

for me today!

let's sing!

Let Us Exalt His Name

Chorus
Glorify, glorify the Lord with me!
Glorify, glorify the Lord with me!
Let us exalt His name together!
Let us exalt His name forever!
Glorify, glorify the Lord with me!
Glorify the Lord, our Lord!

In everything you say, glorify the Lord!
Every night and day, glorify the Lord!
In all that you do, let His glory show through!
Oh, glorify the Lord with me!

(Repeat chorus)

Y

You are my hiding place; you will protect me from trouble.
Psalm 32:7

Sometimes when you've had a really rough day, you'd like to find a hiding place. A place where no one can find you. A safe place where you can rest. A shelter from the storm. Maybe it's in a secret room no one knows about. Or maybe at the top of a tree in your yard. Everyone needs a hiding place sometimes.

Hannah Made a Promise

(Around 1070 B.C.)

Hannah was married to a man named Elkanah. But she was unable to have children. Other mothers teased her until she cried and could not eat. She needed a hiding place. So Hannah went to the temple and fell before the Lord and prayed. She promised the Lord that if He gave her a son, she would give the child back to Him. Eli the priest blessed her before she went home. And in time, the Lord answered her prayer. Her son Samuel was born. Hannah had found comfort in the Lord. He was her hiding place.

The Lord is your hiding place. With Him you can feel safe from your enemies. You can feel secure. He will guard and protect you.

If you are afraid, He calms you. If you are sad, He lifts you up. When you feel like you need a safe haven, don't run in panic. Run to your hiding place, the Lord.

for me today!

let's sing!

You Are My Hiding Place

You, You are my hiding place.
You will protect me from trouble all my days.
You, You are my hiding place.
You will protect me, oh, my Lord.
Love me, hold me, touch me, comfort me.
Love me, hold me, Lord.
Touch me with Your Spirit voice.
I hear it.

(Repeat)

Z

It is not good to have ZEAL without knowledge.

Proverbs 19:2

She'd never had any training.

In fact, she'd never been ice-skating in her life.

But how hard could it be? Put on the skates and glide across the ice. Easy! As they approached the ice, she watched a couple twirling and spinning in the center of the rink. So she jumped onto the ice, and went slipping and sliding out of control! Again and again she tried. Again and again she ended up sprawled on all fours. As much as she wanted to twirl and spin on the ice, she just didn't have the training to do it.

109

Peter Had Great Zeal

(Around A.D. 30)

After Jesus finished praying in the Garden of Gethsemene, a mob came carrying torches and clubs. Led by Judas, they had come to take Jesus away. In his zeal, Peter took his sword and cut off the ear of one of the guards. "Put your sword away!" said Jesus. (John 18:11) Then He reached out and healed the man's ear. Peter had great zeal, but he did not understand that this was God's plan for Jesus.

You can read
this story in
John, chapter 18!

To do things **the right way, you must have** the desire *and* the knowledge to do it. If you desire to play the piano, you must have a knowledge of music to play beautiful melodies. **To act without** knowledge can be very dangerous and embarrassing.

Peter acted without knowledge. He did not know that God had a bigger plan . . . a plan of salvation. Think before you act!

for me today!

let's sing!

Zeal without Knowledge

<u>Chorus</u>
Zeal, zeal, zeal,
Without knowledge, it is not good to have
Zeal, zeal, zeal.
Without knowledge, it is not good to have.

If you don't know how to do it,
Ask a friend.
Get some friendly advice.
If you don't know how to do it,
Don't pretend you do,
Or you might do it all wrong.

(Repeat chorus)

If you don't know how to sing it,
Ask a friend.
Get some friendly advice.
If you don't know how to sing it,
Don't pretend you do,
Or you might sing it all wrong.

And we know that in all things God works for the good of those who love him.

Romans 8:28

Have you ever had to work very hard for something you wanted really badly? Practicing for a recital can be tiring! Studying for a test can be brain-bending! Learning to ride a bike can be painful! But you keep on trying because you know something good is going to come from all of that hard work. Then, when you finally play your song perfectly, ace the test, or zoom around the block on your bike, you know it was all worth it!

The Crucifixion of Jesus

(Around A.D. 30)

Jesus knew that all things work together for good—even when He was hung on the cross to die.

Although it was the saddest day ever, Jesus knew that something good was about to happen.

He knew the world would soon be rejoicing.  And three days later, all things did work together for good. He arose! And the sins of all who love Him were forgiven.

You can read this story in
the Book of Matthew, chapter 27:32
through chapter 28;
Mark, chapters 15 and 16;
and Luke, chapters 23 and 24!

God has given a promise:

All things will work together for

the good of those who love Him.

So no matter what happens, keep trusting

in Jesus! He loves you so much that He died

to save you. He will work for the good in your life.

In All Things

Chorus
And we know that in all things,
God works for the good of those who love Him.
And we know that in all things,
God works for the good of those who love Him.

God has given a promise,
And I know it is true.
All things are working together
For the good of those who believe. Do you?

(Repeat chorus)

God has given a promise.
I will trust in the Lord!
All things are working together
Whether good or bad. In my heart I'm sure . . .

(Repeat chorus)

"How beautiful are the feet of those who bring good news!"

Romans 10:15

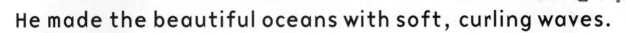

God has made so many beautiful things.

He made the beautiful oceans with soft, curling waves.

He made the beautiful blue skies where birds can

soar. He gave people beautiful voices to sing

praises to Him. But have you heard of beautiful *feet*?

The Bible says that those who tell others about

Jesus have "beautiful feet!"

Paul Was a Missionary

Bible Story

Paul was a missionary. Missionaries can travel far to tell others about Jesus. When Paul traveled to many different places, he would usually walk. Wherever he walked, he told everyone the Good News about God's love. They called his message beautiful. And since his feet brought him there, they called his feet beautiful, too!

His feet brought the beautiful message of God's grace.

You can read about how Paul became a missionary in the Book of Acts, chapter 6!

119

for me today!

You don't have to travel far to find someone who has not heard about Jesus. Many of your friends may have never heard the Good News of God's love. So wherever you go, be sure to tell everyone about Jesus. Your message will be a beautiful message. And the feet that brought you will be beautiful too!

let's sing!

How Beautiful

Chorus
How beautiful are the feet
Of those who bring Good News!
How beautiful are the feet
Of those who bring Good News!

(Repeat chorus)

You don't have to travel far.
This world has plenty of people.
No matter where they are,
The Gospel makes a heart fly,
Higher than a blue sky.

(Repeat chorus)

So wherever you go, my friend,
Tell them the story of Jesus,
How He forgave their sin.
Then you'll be a missionary,
Quite extraordinary!

(Repeat chorus)

"Let the little Children come to me."
Matthew 19:14

Sometimes being a kid can feel less important than being a grownup. You're too young to drive a car. You're too little to ride the Screamin' Demon at the park. And grownups are always saying "be quiet" or "not now" or "hurry up."

It's tough being a kid!

Jesus and the Children

(Around A.D. 30)

Jesus thought children were very important.

He always had time for them. Once, His disciples thought

He was too busy to meet the children.

But when Jesus saw their eager smiles, He said,

"Let the little children come to Me . . . for the kingdom

of heaven belongs to such as these." (Matthew 19:14)

Jesus loves children!

You can read this story in Matthew, chapter 19!

Children are important to God!

Jesus wants children everywhere to know about His special love for them.

What you learn as a child will stay with you as you grow up, giving you many years to learn from and grow closer to God. Jesus thinks you are awesome!

So have a great day being an awesome child of the best Father of all—God.

for me today!

let's sing!

Let the Little Children Come

Chorus
Let 'em, won't you let 'em?
Let the little children come to Me.
Let 'em, won't you let 'em?
Let the little children come to Me.

Jesus loved all the little children.
Jesus, He loved them every one.
Jesus loved all the little children.
He said let the little children come.

(Repeat chorus)

Jesus had time for all the children.
Jesus had time to laugh and play.
Jesus had time for all the children.
He said come to Me, everyone.

(Repeat chorus)

d

"do to others what you would have them do to you."

Matthew 7:12

It takes real courage to be nice.

If you were the only person living on the

planet, you wouldn't have to worry about being nice.

There would be no one to disagree with you.

You wouldn't have to be patient. You wouldn't have

to share with anyone. But look around.

There are 6 billion people on this planet. So, you'll

have to be able to get along with others.

The best way to do that is to treat others the way

you want to be treated.

Joseph and His Brothers

(Around 1900 B.C.)

Bible Story

Joseph's older brothers did not treat him the way *they* wanted to be treated. They were jealous of Joseph and decided to do a terrible thing. They tricked him and sold him to an Egyptian merchant. He was taken to Egypt, far away from his home in Israel.

Years later, when a famine came to Israel, Joseph's brothers went to Egypt to buy food. Guess who was in charge of the food? That's right: Joseph! But he did not return their unkindness.

He loved them and took care of them.

Treating others the way you would like to be treated is called "The Golden Rule." It is golden because of its great value. It creates a world where people of all races and nationalities can live in peace together. It's also golden because those who follow the rule will shine like gold. Starting today, try to treat others just like you want them to treat you!

for me today!

Do to Others

Chorus
Do, do to others what you
Would have them do to you, to you.
Do, do to others what you
Would have them do to you, to you.

(Repeat chorus)

It's gonna take courage to make
This world better, this world better.
If you wanna be nicely treated, hear me.
Be nice, be nice to everyone else.

It's gonna take a hero to make
This world better, this world better.
But you, you can be a hero, you see.
Be nice, be nice if you wanna be treated nice.

"everyone who calls on the name of the Lord will be saved."

Romans 10:13

If you saw an accident and needed to get help fast, who would you call?

Would you call the pizza delivery man? Or the plumber? Of course not! You'd call 9-1-1 and get the emergency medical team on its way. There may be days when you feel bad or sad or upset. That's when you need to remember who to call.

Call upon the Lord!

Jesus Heals the Blind Man

(Around A.D. 30)

One day Jesus was passing through Jericho. A blind man heard the noise of the crowds and wondered what was happening. He could not see. His friends told him that Jesus had come to Jericho. The blind man knew he needed help if he was ever going to see. He shouted, "Jesus . . . have mercy on me!" (Luke 18:38)

Jesus heard the blind man calling His name. Jesus answered and healed him.

The blind man could see!

131

It is very important to know who to call when you need help.

The blind man knew that only Jesus could give him sight. So, he called upon the name of the Lord. He was saved from his blindness.

You can call upon the name of the Lord and be saved from danger, bullies, temptation, and even your sin.

He will help you today. Just call on Him!

Everyone Who Calls on the Name of the Lord

Chorus
Everyone, everyone, everyone,
Who calls on the name of the Lord,
They will be saved forever,
Everyone who calls,
Everyone who calls,
On the name of the Lord.

When trouble comes to call,
You're just about to fall,
Call on the name of the Lord.
When people are unkind,
A friend is hard to find,
Call on the Lord.

(Repeat chorus)

When sickness comes to stay,
You need a brighter day,
Call on the name of the Lord.
When sadness fills your heart,
Tears about to start,
Call on the Lord.

(Repeat chorus)

forgive as the Lord forgave you.

Colossians 3:13

It is important always to treat others with kindness.

That seems like an easy thing to do, right?

Well, it is easy until someone is mean to *you*.

That's when you have to make a choice. Do you return meanness for meanness? Do you hold a grudge?

No! There's a better choice.

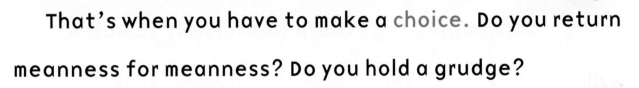

You can learn to forgive!

133

Peter Learns to Forgive

(Around A.D. 29)

Peter once came to Jesus.

He wanted to learn to forgive. So he asked Jesus,

"How many times shall I forgive my brother when he

sins against me? Up to seven times?" (Matthew 18:21)

Jesus told Peter that he should forgive more than

seven times. He should forgive seven times seventy!

Jesus explained that there was no limit to God's

forgiveness, so Peter should have no limit to his

forgiveness towards others.

If there is ever a time that someone treats you unfairly, learn the lesson Peter learned from Jesus. Forgive that person as the Lord forgave you. Think about the many times you have been forgiven by your heavenly Father.

Then choose to act like Jesus. Forgive!

for me today!

let's sing!

Forgive

We learn to live when we forgive,
Just the way that Jesus did.
We learn to love like God above,
When we can love the ones who shove.
It's not an easy thing to do, child,
But now we have a song for you, child,
Saying to the world, every boy and girl!

Chorus
Forgive a little bit, gonna be like Jesus!
Forgive a little bit, gonna be like Him!
Forgive a little bit, never gonna quit livin' for Him!
Forgive a little bit, as the Lord forgave you!
Forgive a little bit, gonna be like Him!
We learn to live when we forgive,
We forgive.

We learn to care when we forbear
Unkind words, a call unfair.
We learn to grow, God's love we show,
When we forgive and let it go.
It's not an easy thing to do, child,
But now we have a song for you, child,
Saying to the world, every boy and girl!

(Repeat chorus)

"give, and it will be given to you."

Luke 6:38

Keisha looked at the offering plate. It was coming her way. She reached in her purse and pulled out a quarter. She wanted to give more than that! The plate was full of dollars, checks, and envelopes stuffed with money. She just had twenty-five cents, but she gave it all. Keisha wondered,

What can God do with my little offering?

137

Jesus Feeds Thousands

(Around A.D. 29)

Jesus once made a LOT from a little offering.

He was preaching on a hillside to five thousand people.

When evening came, the people were very hungry.

But there was no food. One boy offered his lunch of five

barley loaves and two small fish to Jesus.

But how far would that go to feed so many?

Jesus blessed the loaves and fish. Then five thousand

people ate dinner and had as much as they wanted.

It was a great miracle!

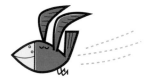

139

A little in God's hands is better than a lot in your own hands. He has promised in the Bible that if you are willing to give unselfishly to others, He is willing to give back to you an even greater blessing. Imagine a blessing so big that your house wouldn't be able to hold it. It's nice to know that you can never 'outgive' God! Be a happy giver!

Give

Chorus
Jesus said:
Give and it will be given to you.
Jesus said:
Give and it will be given to you.

We must understand
That a little in God's hand
Is truly better than
A lot in our own.
We must understand
There's a blessing from His hand
If we give a hungry man
What he needs—this we believe!

(Repeat chorus)

We must understand,
Oh, that giving is God's plan,
And all across our land
Lift our voice and sing.
People understand
That a selfish heart is bland,
But a giving heart is grand.
So let's give, and learn to live!

h:

"**The Lord is my helper; I will not be afraid.**"

Hebrews 13:6

THINKIN' 2day

Everyone needs help at one time or another.

Sometimes a problem is just too big for

one person to solve. Sometimes a burden is just too

heavy to carry alone. That's when you need a helper.

Someone who loves you and cares about you.

So, what can you do when you need

help with a problem?

Daniel in the Lions' Den

(Around 539 B.C.)

Daniel had a big problem. The king had made a law that everyone had to pray to *him* and *only him.* But Daniel would only pray to God—not to a person! When Daniel refused to pray to the king, he was thrown into a den of hungry lions. All alone, Daniel was no match for those hungry lions. But the Lord was with him. Daniel called out for help, and God shut the mouths of the lions.

Daniel was saved!

God loves you and cares about you
all the time. You are never out of His sight.
You are always in His hands.
So when trouble comes, remember:
you are not alone. Call on the Lord.
There is no burden too heavy for Him, no problem
He cannot solve. Problems can be big; problems can be small.
But any problem in God's hands is *no* problem at all!

The Lord Is My Helper

Chorus
The Lord is my helper,
The Lord is my helper,
The Lord is my helper,
I will not be afraid.

(Repeat chorus)

God loves the world He made.
God loves you, too!
God knows your every need.
He will help you through.

(Repeat chorus)

God hears your every prayer.
God answers too!
God leads me everywhere.
He will lead you, too!

(Repeat chorus)

"What is impossible with men is possible with God."

Luke 18:27

The doctors came out of the operating room with their heads lowered. They had worked very hard to remove the cancer. The family walked quietly into the hospital room and knelt beside little Zach's bed to pray. "Lord, the doctors said only a miracle can heal him now. We ask You, Lord, to do what is impossible for us to do." The Lord answered their prayers, and Zach got well. He received a miracle!

Sarah Receives a Miracle

(Around 2066 B.C.)

Sarah received a miracle.

She was the wife of Abraham. God had promised them a son. He told Abraham that his descendants would outnumber the stars in the sky. But many years had passed and Abraham was now 100 years old. When the Lord told Abraham it was time to have a son, Sarah laughed. *Impossible,* she thought. *We're too old!* But, one year later, a little baby boy was born. Their impossible dream was named Isaac.

You can read the whole story in Genesis, chapter 18!

Is anything too hard for the Lord?

Whether it's healing the sick or

keeping His promise that a baby will be born,

God can do it! Let these words

encourage you: Your God can!

He can do what no man can do.

All things are possible in the hands of Almighty God.

What Is Impossible with Men

Chorus
What is impossible with men,
Is possible with God!
No matter what the odds may be,
In Christ I find my victory!
What is impossible with men,
Is possible with God, my friend!
Through it all, come thick or thin,
I'll believe, it's possible with Him.

Too hard? Nothing can be
Too hard if you believe.
God will answer me,
If I pray and I believe.

(Repeat chorus)

Too big? Is anything
Too big for Jesus our King?
Nothing He cannot do,
Just believe, God's Word is true.

(Repeat chorus)

"Jesus answered,... "You must be born again."

John 3:5–7

THINKIN'
2day

One summer day, Shelby and her family headed to the amusement park. As they reached the ticket booth, the man behind the counter waved Shelby and her little sister through. But he stopped their parents at the gate. "I'm sorry," he said, "but to enter, you must turn into a child." Shelby's mom and dad exchanged confused looks. "But sir," Mom began, "we're adults. There's no way we can turn back into children."

The man burst into laughter. "I don't mean your age. Only the young at heart can enter here!" Shelby's parents looked at each other again and smiled. "Oh, we can be *like* children," they said. And they entered the gates.

Nicodemus

(Around A.D. 27)

Nicodemus had heard Jesus teach.

He had seen the miracles Jesus had done. But when Jesus spoke of being born again, Nicodemus was confused. "How can a man be born when he is old?"

Nicodemus asked. Jesus explained that he was speaking of a spiritual birth. Just as we are born physically, we must also be born spiritually if we want to enter heaven. This happens when we say "no" to sin, turn from it, and say "yes" to Jesus.

Remember, no one can enter the kingdom of heaven unless he is born again.

You can read
about Nicodemus
in John, chapter 3.

151

How can you be born again?

Baby fish can only be born from fish.

Baby birds can only be born from birds.

And a new spirit can only be born from the

for me today!

Holy Spirit. When you ask Jesus to come into

your heart, you are born again spiritually. And as

babies depend on their parents, you will then depend on your

heavenly Father. When you get hungry, the Bible will encourage

you. When you are weak, God will make you strong. You will be

a new person. You will be born again. And you will be able to

enter the kingdom of God!

let's sing!

Jesus Said

Jesus said, "You must be born again."
Jesus said, "You must be born again."
Jesus said, "You must be born again."
Gonna ask Him into my heart!
Gonna ask Him today, ask Him to stay!
Gonna ask Him to be the Lord of me!

Jesus said, "You must be born again."
Jesus said, "You must be born again."
Jesus said, "You must be born again."
Gonna ask Him into my heart!
Tell Him my cares, tell Him my prayers!
Ask Him to stay with me all the way!

K

Always try to be kind to each other and to everyone else.

1 Thessalonians 5:15

THINKIN' 2day

It was Marcia's first day at school. She had moved from Costa Rica and spoke very little English.

She was nervous and quite shy. As class ended, Marcia stood alone. One girl walked over and said, "Hi, Marcia. My name is Wendy. Welcome to our school!"

Marcia's face lit up with a bright, beautiful smile.

"Thank you," she answered. Marcia and Wendy began to talk, and before long, Marcia had invited Wendy over to swim in her pool!

Ruth and Naomi

(Between 1210 B.C. and 1050 B.C.)

Ruth and her mother-in-law, Naomi, lived

together in a place far from Naomi's home. Both Naomi's

and Ruth's husbands had died. One day, Naomi

decided that it was time to return to her homeland.

But Ruth loved Naomi and did not want her to go alone.

Ruth knew exactly what to do. She told Naomi,

"Every place you go, I will go." (Ruth 1:16 ICB)

Ruth left her home and traveled many miles to

Judah to be with Naomi. God soon blessed Ruth for her

kindness to Naomi. There Ruth met a man named Boaz,

and they were married.

Sometimes God whispers to your heart,

"Say a kind word to the visitor,"

or "Go visit the elderly lady across

the street." Being kind is a choice we make.

It is also one of the fruits of the Spirit

mentioned in the Bible. When you pray,

ask God to give you a spirit of kindness.

Then treat it like peanut butter: spread it around!

Try to Be Kind

Sometimes God is calling you, child.
Sometimes He's got a job to do.
One of His children may be in despair,
And a little kindness you could surely share.

Chorus
Always, always try to be kind.
Always, always try to be kind,
To each other, sister and brother,
To everyone, to everyone else,
Be kind.

Sometimes we don't want to listen.
Sometimes when God is calling us,
But one of His children's waiting there.
Maybe one day you might need some kindness, too.

1

"For God so loved the world that he gave his one and only Son, that whoever believes in him shall not perish but have eternal life."

John 3:16

THINKIN'
2day

When you love somebody,

you want to make that person happy.

Giving a gift is a great way to make someone happy.

When you spend your time, money, or effort to create a

gift for someone, you show that you really care.

A gift says "I love you" in a special way.

God So Loved the World

Bible Story

(The book of John was written between A.D. 80 and A.D. 90. Christ was crucified in the Spring of A.D. 30.)

God said "I love you" to the whole world. And He did it in a very special way. Your loving God, whose power has no limits, whose strength cannot be measured, your God who knows all things, gave a very special gift to you. He gave His one and only Son, Jesus, to die on the cross. Because of that gift, your sins can be forgiven and you can have eternal life!

159

There are many kinds of gifts, big and small. Some have great value.

God's gift to you has a greater value than anyone could ever imagine— a gift of eternal life. This gift allows you to live forever in heaven. But it came at a great cost.

It cost Jesus His life. Receive this gift with great joy. It's God's gift of love to the world—and to you!

for me today!

let's sing!

For God So Loved the World

For God so loved the world,
For God so loved the world,
For God so loved the world,
That He gave His one and only Son.

That whoever believes in Him
Shall not perish
But have everlasting life.
Whoever believes in Him
Will have it, will have it
Will have everlasting life.

(Repeat)

m

"Be merciful, just as your Father is merciful."

Luke 6:36

Brittany had worked so hard on her homework assignment. *How could she have left for school without it?* It was due today and it counted as half her grade. She was nearly in tears when she walked up to her teacher's desk. "Mr. Rhymer, I'm sorry, but I forgot my homework. I really did it, and I worked so hard." Mr. Rhymer forgave her and said, "You've been a wonderful student, Brittany. Could you bring it tomorrow?"

161

The Unmerciful Servant

(Around A.D. 28)

Jesus spoke of a servant who asked for mercy. He owed the king a lot of money. But he could not pay the debt. The servant begged for mercy, "Be patient . . . and I will pay back everything." (Matthew 18:26)

The king showed great mercy and forgave the servant's debt. But that same servant found another man who owed him money. He, too, begged for mercy. But no mercy was shown. The servant had the man who was in debt to him thrown into prison. When the king heard what the evil servant had done, he was very angry.

Justice is getting what you deserve.

Mercy is getting something good

that you do *not* deserve. We can learn

to show mercy by doing the thing Jesus did.

He had mercy upon the sick, the dying, even *you*.

Everyone who sins deserves death. But because of Jesus,

you are given mercy. Sometimes, the thing you don't deserve is

the thing you need the most!

Be Merciful

Chorus
Be merciful, be merciful, be merciful,
Just as your Father is merciful.
Be merciful, be merciful, be merciful,
Just as your Father is merciful.

Mercy me, Lord! I hope You'll be, Lord,
Merciful to me.
Mercy me, Lord!
I do believe, Lord,
Mercy and grace we all do need.

(Repeat chorus)

Mercy me, Lord! How can it be, Lord?
You're merciful to me.
Mercy me, Lord! Together we, Lord,
Praise You for mercy!
And it's how we wanna be,

(Repeat chorus)

n

"Love your neighbor as yourself."

Matthew 19:19

THINKIN' 2day

Rosa had never seen snow falling the way it did on that day. She tried to catch snowflakes on her tongue as she walked with her dad toward the mall. As they made their last turn, Rosa saw a homeless man huddled on the sidewalk. He had no coat. Without saying a word, her father took off his coat and covered the man. Then he said, "I'll pay for your room tonight at that motel," pointing across the street. Rosa has never forgotten that moment.

The Good Samaritan

(Around A.D. 28)

Jesus once told a parable about a man traveling from Jerusalem to Jericho. The man was robbed, beaten, and left lying on the side of the road. A passing priest saw the man, but did nothing to help him. Next, another helper from the church passed by, but he, too, did nothing. Then came a Samaritan. He stopped and cared for the man. He bandaged his wounds and took him to an inn and even paid for the room himself.

After Jesus told the story, He asked, "Which of these three do you think was a neighbor . . . ?" (Luke 10:36) Surely it was the one who

met the needs of the hurting!

You can read
the whole story
in Luke, chapter 10!

So, who is *your* neighbor?

Your neighbor is anyone who has a need that you can meet. You don't have to look very hard to find people with needs in the world. Perhaps in your own family, school, or church, you know someone who could use a visit or a cheerful word.

Just think: if you love your neighbor as yourself, God can change the entire neighborhood!

for me today!

let's sing!

Love Your Neighbor

<u>Chorus</u>
Love your neighbor.
Love your neighbor as yourself.
Love your neighbor.
Love your neighbor as yourself.
Who is my neighbor?
Anyone who has a need!
So just love your neighbor,
And that's the way it's s'posed to be.

We don't have to look too far.
Love your neighbor.
Find a need wherever we are.
Love your neighbor.
Speak a word; lend a hand.
Love your neighbor, understand.

(Repeat chorus)

Someone in your school today,
Love your neighbor
Is feelin' down and so I say,
Love your neighbor
Here's a chance to be a friend.
Let a better day begin.

168

(Repeat chorus)

Children, **Obey** your parents in the Lord.

Ephesians 6:1

Tasha didn't always obey the first time she was told to do something. Many times, her mother would have to ask two or three times before she would obey. One day she and her mother were kicking a soccer ball in the front yard. With one kick, it rolled into the street. Without paying attention to the passing car, Tasha ran into the street. "Tasha, stop!" her mother shouted. *Honk! Screech!* The car barely missed hitting her! Learning to obey the first time is a very good habit.

Jonah and the Whale

(Around 785 B.C.)

Poor Jonah had to learn to obey the hard way.

God told Jonah to go to Nineveh and preach.

Jonah didn't want to so he sailed the other way.

God sent a terrible storm which tossed the big

ship up and down. Jonah knew the storm was his fault.

He told the sailors, "Throw me into the sea . . . and it will

become calm." (Jonah 1:12) Jonah was tossed overboard

and . . . GULP! He was swallowed by a great, big fish.

For three days, Jonah was inside the belly of that fish

as it swam through the ocean. He promised God, "I will

obey this time." The fish spit him out on dry land.

Jonah finally obeyed and went to Nineveh!

Tasha was almost hurt because she did not obey her mother the first time.

for me today!

Jonah spent three very unpleasant days inside a big fish because he did not obey his heavenly Father the first time. Learning to obey your parents is a very important sign of growing up.

Your parents have wisdom, and God has said in His Word that you should obey your parents. God has *all* wisdom so you should trust and obey Him—the first time!

let's sing!

Children, Obey Your Parents

Children, obey your parents in the Lord,
For this is right.
Children, obey your parents in the Lord,
For this is right.
Honor your father and mother,
Which is the first commandment with a promise
That it may go well with you
And that you may enjoy long life on the earth!

(Repeat)

P

Be Patient, bearing with one another in love.

Ephesians 4:2

Matt really didn't mean to do it.

He had one hand on the glass, one hand on the door.

But when Sparky barked and came bounding through

the door—*splash!*—milk went everywhere. Mom grabbed a

handful of paper towels and said patiently,

"It's just a little spill. It's okay."

Together Mom and Matt cleaned up the milk.

175

The Prodigal Son

(Around A.D. 28)

Jesus tells of a patient father who loved his two sons dearly. The younger one said, "Give me my share of the family inheritance now. I am leaving for a far country." The loving father did as his son had asked. The son moved away and soon wasted all of his money. He became so hungry that he took a job feeding pigs and even ate their food. One day, he came to his senses. *I'll go home and work for my father,* he thought. When he was almost home, his patient father ran to him and hugged him. The boy said, "I am no longer worthy to be called your son. May I work for you?" But his father loved him and celebrated his return!

You can read this story in Luke, chapter 15!

A big part of loving someone is showing patience. Sometimes, you have to put up with things you don't like. No one plants a seed of corn in the ground and comes back the next day asking, "Where's the corn?" You must be patient. Good things take a little time. Today, practice a little patience with your family and friends.

for me today!

let's sing!

Be Patient

You've planted a seed in a garden today.
Be patient, for this we do know.
You've planted a seed,
Now there's coming a day.
Be patient, the flower will grow.

Chorus
Be patient, be patient,
Bearing with one another in love.
Be patient, be patient,
Be patient, the flower will grow.

You've planted a seed in the Lord's holy name.
Be patient for this we do know.
You've planted a seed.
Pray in time for the rain.
Be patient, the flower will grow.

(Repeat chorus)

q

Everyone should be quick to listen, slow to speak and slow to become angry.

James 1:19

Ryan was always talking in class.

As Mr. Myers was passing out the tests, Ryan just

kept on talking. Mr. Myers said, "Listen carefully.

First, read every question, and then begin the test."

Everyone did as Mr. Myers said—everyone except for

Ryan. He wasn't listening. Within minutes, everyone

began to leave the classroom. Ryan wondered how

they could possibly be finished! But then, as

he got to the last question, he read,

"Now go back and only answer question number one."

177

The Parable of the Sower

(Around A.D. 28)

Jesus said, "Listen!" He had something very important to say. He told the story of a farmer who went out to sow some seed. Some seeds fell on the path and birds ate it. Some fell on the rocks and were scorched by the sun. Some fell in thorn bushes and were choked. But some fell on good soil and produced a crop. Jesus explained, "The seed is the Word of God." (Luke 8:11) Some people are like seeds on the path. They hear the Word of God, but Satan comes and takes it away. Some are like seeds on the rocks. They receive the Word but fall away when trials come. Some are like seed sown among thorns. The Word is choked out by worry. But others listen and obey. They receive God's blessings!

You can read
this story
in Luke, chapter 8!

for me today!

It's easier to open your ears if your mouth is closed. When you listen, you can learn. But with so many voices calling out in this world, who should you listen to? The voice of God, of course! He speaks through the Bible. So today, be quick to listen and be slow to speak!

let's sing!

Everyone Should Be Quick to Listen

Chorus
Everyone should be quick to listen.
Everyone should be quick to listen,
Slow to speak and slow to become angry.
Everyone should be quick to listen.
Everyone should be quick to listen,
Slow to speak and that's how it oughta' be!

It's easier to open your ears
If your mouth is closed.
But some are breezier than a hurricane
That blows and blows and blows!

(Repeat chorus)

It's sensible to listen and learn,
So listen now to me!
It's reprehensible—what?—I'll make it clear.
Button those lips and brighter you'll be!

(Repeat chorus)

Show proper respect to everyone.

1 Peter 2:17

"Lightning can be a very dangerous thing," said Mr. Butler. Mr. Butler was a meteorologist. But we call him the weather man. He had come to visit our school. "Lightning is a very powerful bolt of electricity," he explained. "It can strike trees and even people. Hundreds of people each year die because they do not use caution during lightning storms. Yes, lightning is very, very powerful and must be respected."

David and Goliath

(Around 1025 B.C.)

Goliath was a very big and powerful man. But he had a lesson to learn about respecting God! Goliath was a Philistine warrior. He stood over nine feet tall! One day, Israel met the Philistine army for battle. Each morning, for 40 days, Goliath would stand in the valley and shout insults at Israel and their God. He had no respect for them. Goliath was about to find out how powerful God really is!

When David heard Goliath mocking God, he marched out to do battle. Although David was just a boy, his God was mighty! David carried a slingshot with him and said, "I come against you in the name of the LORD." (1 Samuel 17:45) Then he hurled a stone at Goliath. *Bam!* David hit him squarely in the head. Down went the giant! Goliath should have respected God's mighty power!

Be sure to show proper respect for everyone you meet. All people were created by God, made in His image. And for that, they deserve your respect.

You should never disrespect others because of the way they look, the language they speak, or the things they have. If we respect others, they will respect us, too! Peter said to show R-E-S-P-E-C-T to everyone!

for me today!

let's sing!

Show Proper Respect

Chorus
Show proper respect to everyone you meet,
Kids across the street, around the block.
It doesn't stop there.
Show proper respect to everyone you meet—
Big or small, short or tall, doesn't matter at all!
Show proper respect!

R-E-S-P-E-C-T!
We can spell it,
But do we know what it means?
R-E-S-P-E-C-T!
They can tell it
When they see it in you and me.

R-E-S-P-E-C-T!   (Repeat chorus)
We can sing it,
But do we give it away?
R-E-S-P-E-C-T!
When you bring it to the world,
They all shout hooray!

(Repeat chorus)

S

Seek first his kingdom and his righteousness, and all these things will be given to you.

Matthew 6:33

The
End

The Cinema Plaza was fantastic!

There were 20 movies playing in different theatres, all at the same time. "Enjoy *Cartoon Town.* I'll be back at 8:30," Cara's mom called as she watched Cara and Allison walk into the theatre. As the girls passed a movie poster, Allison said, "Hey, Cara, let's go see the scary movie instead. No one will know." Cara knew her mom trusted her to do what's right, and she didn't want to let her down. "Nah, *Cartoon Town* is just fine with me," Cara replied, and she stepped up

tickets

to the ticket booth.

Shadrach, Meshach, and Abednego

(Around 580 B.C.)

Shadrach, Meshach, and Abednego knew that God trusted them to do what was right.

So when the king set up a statue and told all his governors to worship it, Shadrach, Meshach, and Abednego refused. They knew that one day they would answer to God, who was greater than any king. The king ordered them to be thrown into a fiery furnace. They told the king "God . . . is able to save us . . . But even if He does not, . . . we will not serve your gods." (Daniel 3:17–18) Into the fire they went.

But they were not burned. They didn't even smell like smoke. God saved them because they obeyed Him!

186

You can read the whole story in Daniel, chapter 3!

Cara had been trusted to do the right thing. She knew that if she disobeyed her mother, her mother would no longer trust her. She would answer to her mother, not her friend. That's how it is when we're tempted to disobey the Lord. Who will you answer to? The friends who are tempting you or the Lord? That's right! Just remember, seek His righteousness first!

for me today!

let's sing!

Seek First His Kingdom

Seek first His kingdom
And His righteousness.
Seek first His kingdom
And all these things will be given to you,
All these things will be given to you.

Joy will be given to you.
Peace will be given to you.
Love will be given to you,
If we will seek the kingdom of God!
If we will seek the kingdom of God!

(Repeat)

"Whoever can be trusted with very little can also be trusted with much."

Luke 16:10

THINKIN' 2day

"Mr. President, what was your very first public office?" asked the fifth grader.

The President was visiting a middle school in Nashville, Tennessee. "Now, that's a very good question," responded the President. "My very first public office was held at Dunbar Elementary School, where I was elected treasurer of Mrs. Casto's sixth-grade class. The other students trusted me to collect and turn in the

 lunch money each day."

The Parable of the Talents

(Around A.D. 30)

A master once trusted his servants with his money. To one, he gave five thousand dollars. To another, he gave two thousand, and to another, he gave one thousand. Then the master went on a long journey. When he returned, he called the three servants in for a report. The one with five thousand had gained five thousand more. The one with two thousand had gained two thousand more.

"Well done," said the master. "You have been faithful with a few things; I will put you in charge of many things!" But the man with one thousand dollars had gained nothing. He could not be trusted again!

To get a big job with big responsibility, you must first show that you can be trusted to do little jobs. The President didn't start by managing a whole country. He started with a small job in the sixth grade.

Trust is something you earn every day. If you are faithful to complete the little jobs around the house, then you show everyone you are ready for bigger and more important jobs. Doing a little job well can lead to BIG things!

for me today!

let's sing!

Whoever Can Be Trusted

Whoever, whoever, whoever,
Whoever can be trusted,
Whoever, whoever, whoever,
Whoever can be trusted,
With very little
I know it's true!
Can also be trusted with much
Can you?
Whoever, whoever, whoever,
Whoever can be trusted...
You want a big job.
You want a big job.
So do the little job right
To show you're in the know!
You're responsible!

(Repeat)

U

Do not let any Unwholesome talk come out of your mouths, but only what is helpful for building others up.

Ephesians 4:29

THINKIN' 2day

The football stadium was packed. Spirits were high, and the team had played their hearts out. It was tied, 31 to 31, with three seconds left on the clock. The ball was snapped. The kick went up. "No good!" shouted the referee. In the stands behind Marcus and his dad, they heard a young man yelling a lot of really bad words! Dad turned to the young man, "Your bad words won't affect the score, but they do affect others around you!"

Job Faces Many Trials

(Around 2000 B.C.)

Job faced many trials, yet no unwholesome talk came out of his mouth. Satan was allowed to take his ten children. But Job didn't sin in what he said. Satan was allowed to take all of Job's possessions. But Job didn't sin in what he said. Satan was allowed to make Job sick. Even when Job's wife told him to curse God and die, he didn't sin. In all of his troubles, Job did not speak unkind words to God.

Your tongue is like a rudder on a ship—small with a big purpose—and, it must be controlled. It must not speak words that are unwholesome. Those words may hinder others from seeing Jesus. Always speak good words that encourage, no matter what happens. Speaking bad words won't change anything. But a good word, spoken at just the right time, can change everything!

for me today!

let's sing!

Unwholesome Talk

Do not, do-do-do not
Do-do-do not let any, let any,
Do not, do-do-do not
Do-do-do not let any, let any,
Do not, do-do-do not,
Do-do-do not let any, let any,
Unwholesome talk
Come out of your ma-ma-ma mouth!
Ma-ma-ma mouth!
But only what
Only what
Only what is helpful for
Building others uppity!
But only what
Only what
Only what is helpful for
Building others uppity, uppity, uppity, uppity!

196

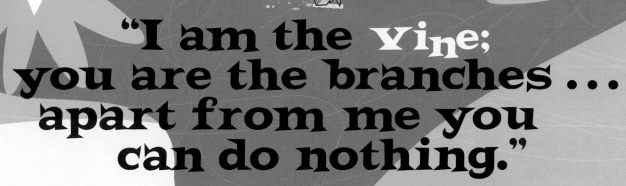

"I am the vine; you are the branches ... apart from me you can do nothing."

John 15:5

The thunder was getting louder and louder.

Suddenly, a bolt of lightning lit up the entire night sky.

Boom! went the thunder; then the lights went out.

"Turn on the lights!" cried Bobby, John's little 4-year-old brother. "We didn't turn the lights off, Bobby," John's mom explained in a comforting voice.

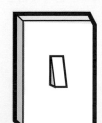

"When the electric power is off, the lights won't work."

Samson, the Strongest Man

(Around 1050 B.C.)

Bible Story

Samson's source of power was the Lord. Before Samson was born, an angel came to Samson's mother. The angel told her that her baby would be blessed with the gift of strength in order to do God's work. The angel explained that Samson's hair was never to be cut. She followed the angel's instructions, and Samson soon grew to be the strongest man in the world. He defeated over a thousand men using the jawbone of a donkey! Later, Samson fell in love with a woman named Delilah. Delilah didn't believe in God. When Samson told her the secret of his strength, she told his secret to the enemy, and the enemy cut off his hair. He was powerless!

Your source of strength is the Lord.
He is like a vine that feeds all the branches.
The branches then feed the grapes.
If the grape is cut off from the vine,
   it dies. Likewise, if you cut yourself
off from the Lord, you lose your source of strength.
   You can do nothing. You are powerless like Samson. But, if
you stay attached to Jesus, you're like a lamp that has the
   electricity on . . . you shine! You can do all things through
      Christ who strengthens you.

for me today!

let's sing!

I Am the Vine

Chorus
I, I, I, I am the vine.
I, I, I, I am the vine.
You, you, you, you are the branches.
But I, I, I, I am the vine.
Apart from Me you can do nothing.
Apart, you see, you can do nothing.
I, I, I, I am the vine.

   Our Lord has power to spare.
   See His power everywhere.
   Our Lord, gives power to me.
   Without Him I'm nothing, you see.

   (Repeat chorus)

   Our Lord can do all things.
   He made the diamond in a diamond ring.
   His power is great, you see.
   Without Him, what would I be?

   (Repeat chorus)

200

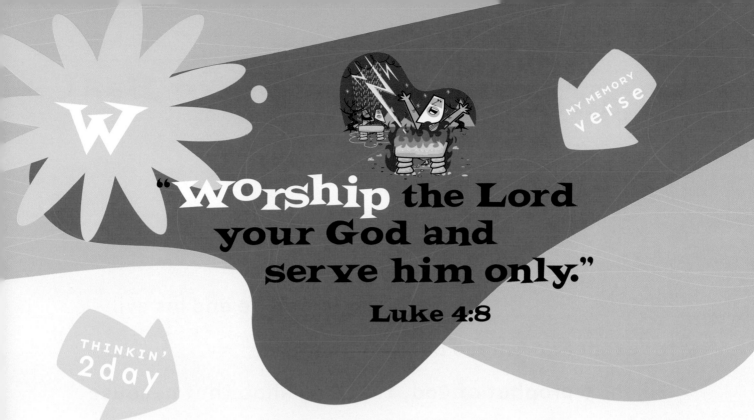

"Worship the Lord your God and serve him only."

Luke 4:8

"How can it be true?" asked the lieutenant.

"Are you 100% positive?" Yes, it was true.

Marcus Johnson was a double agent.

For years, he had been working as a spy for the United States. Now he was working for the enemy.

He was selling secrets to other countries! Marcus was arrested, tried in court, and found guilty of treason.

You cannot serve two countries.

Marcus had betrayed his country.

Elijah and the Prophets of Baal

(Around 850 B.C.)

Wicked King Ahab ruled in Israel. He and his evil wife Jezebel worshiped Baal, a false god.

Elijah, a prophet of God, told King Ahab that because of his wickedness, it would not rain until Elijah said it would. Elijah challenged the prophets of Baal to meet him on Mt. Carmel. Elijah instructed them to get two bulls to lay on an altar. He told them, "Call on the name of your god, and I will call on the name of the LORD. The god who answers by fire— He is the one true God."(1 Kings 18:24) The prophets of Baal called on their god. Nothing happened. They called again and again. Nothing happened. But when Elijah called on the true God, fire fell from heaven, and then the rains began to fall! Everyone then knew who the true God really was.

The Bible is clear: Worship the Lord and serve Him only. You cannot serve two masters. That's like being a double agent. You will always favor one or the other. You must serve God and Him alone.

The "gods" of this world offer things that begin with a little "g". Things like gold and things that glitter.

But the true God offers you things that begin with a big "G". Things like Grace and Goodness!

Serve the "big G" God!

for me today!

let's sing!

Worship the Lord

Oh, worship the Lord your God!
Oh, worship the Lord your God!
Oh, worship the Lord your God,
And serve Him only.

Oh, honor the Lord your God!
Oh, honor the Lord your God!
Oh, honor the Lord your God,
And serve Him only.

Give praise to the Lord your God!
Give praise to the Lord your God!
Give praise to the Lord your God,
And serve Him only.

MY MEMORY **verse**

If anything is eXcellent or praiseworthy — think about such things.

Philippians 4:8

THINKIN' **2day**

Aa
Bb
Cc

Mrs. Johnson had an excellent class,

twenty of the most well-mannered kids you'd ever find.

She set the standard very high. She expected

excellence in all of their subjects, and she

expected excellence in their behavior.

When they met her standard,

they were excellent!

Moses Receives the Ten Commandments

(Around 1445 B.C.)

God listed His standards for excellence in the Ten Commandments. When Moses received the  Ten Commandments from God, the Lord said, "I am the LORD your God, who brought you out of Egypt." (Exodus 20:2) These Ten Commandments were, and still are, God's standard of excellent behavior for every boy and girl. They teach His people how to treat each other and how to honor God. They also help us see why we need a Savior.

God sets the standard very high!

You can read this story in Exodus, chapter 20!

A steering wheel controls a car.

But what controls the mind?

What you put into it! If something is excellent in God's eyes, you should think about it. If something is worthy of praise, you should think about it. But there are Web sites, television shows, movies, and magazines that are not excellent or praiseworthy in God's sight.

Don't give them a second thought!

Seek God's kind of excellence!

for me today!

let's sing!

If Anything Is Excellent

Chorus
Do, do, do, do, do, do, do, do, do, do, do, do!
If anything is excellent,
If anything is praiseworthy,
If anything is excellent or praiseworthy,
Think about such things!

Think about His love, His grace,
That wonderful place we all call heaven,
Seven days a week!
Think about His love, His joy,
Every girl and boy
Come on!
Think about His love every day! Hear me say,
Think about His love every day, every day!

(Repeat chorus)

Y

Don't let anyone look down on you because you are young, but set an example for the believers in speech, in life, in love, in faith and in purity.

1 Timothy 4:12

THINKIN' 2day

Celebrities can have a great influence on many people. They set examples that many will follow. If they are polite and you see that example, perhaps you will be polite. If they wear their hair a

certain way or dress a certain way, a lot of people will follow. You, too, can influence the people around you with your actions. And others can learn from your example.

Paul, a Good Example

(Around 55 A.D.)

Paul wrote a letter to the church at Corinth. In it, he makes a remarkable statement. It is one that few of us would dare make. He said, "Follow my example, as I follow the example of Christ."

(1 Corinthians 11:1) Paul was learning and obeying the teachings of Jesus and living them out in his daily life. His speech, love, and faith showed the world, he was a Christian!

211

Is your life a good example of the Christian life? As a believer, you need to set a good example. Your speech needs to be clean and pure. Your life needs to be free from sinful habits. And your faith should be growing. Even though you are young, you can set a good example for others. You're never too young to be a good example!

let's sing!

Because You Are Young

Don't let anyone
Don't let anyone
Look down on you.
Don't let anyone
Don't let anyone
Look down on you
Because, because, because you are young.
No! Don't let anyone
Don't let anyone
Look down on you,
But set an example for believers in life.
Set an example for believers in love.
Set an example for believers in faith.
And don't let anyone,
No, not anyone, look down on you.

"Zacchaeus, come down immediately."

Luke 19:5

When you're a kid living in an adult world, it can be very frustrating. For instance, you're watching the Christmas parade pass by. Suddenly, there's a really exciting moment.  christmas All the adults jump up to watch. You can't see anything. You're not tall enough. Sometimes, you wish you could just take a ladder to the parade.

Then you could see!

213

Zacchaeus Sees Jesus

(Around A.D. 30)

Once, Jesus passed through Jericho on

His way to Jerusalem. Jericho was the home of Zacchaeus,

a tax collector. Zacchaeus wanted to see Jesus,

but he was very short. He could not see over the crowds.

So, he climbed up in a sycamore tree. From there,

he could see. When Jesus passed by, He saw Zacchaeus

and said, "Come down immediately. I must stay at

your house today." (Luke 19:5) Zacchaeus welcomed

Jesus and was saved.

You can read
this story in
Luke, chapter 19!

215

Do you want to see Jesus?

Zacchaeus did! He wasn't going to let

anything stand in his way.

So, don't let anything stand in your way.

You're not too young; you're not too old.

You can't be too short or tall, fat or thin.

If you want to see Jesus, you can find Him.

He's looking for you!

for me today!

let's sing!

Zacchaeus

Zacchaeus was a wee little man.
A wee little man was he.
How will I ever see Jesus?
He climbed up in a sycamore tree,
For the Lord he wanted to see.
Now I can see Jesus!
And as the Lord passed by his way,
He looked up in the tree.
Jesus can see me!
And Jesus said, "Zacchaeus come down immediately!"
Immediately?
"Immediately!
"I must stay at your house today.
"I must stay at your house today."

26 Old Testament Verses

	Memory Verse	Reference	Page
A	How awesome is the LORD Most High.	Psalm 47:2	9
B	On my bed I remember you; I think of you through the watches of the night.	Psalm 63:6	13
C	God created the heavens and the earth.	Genesis 1:1	17
D	My mouth will declare your praise.	Psalm 51:15	21
E	Let everything that has breath praise the LORD.	Psalm 150:6	25
F	A friend loves at all times.	Proverbs 17:17	29
G	A gentle answer turns away wrath.	Proverbs 15:1	33
H	Love the LORD your God with all your heart and with all your soul and with all your strength.	Deuteronomy 6:5	37
I	So God created man in his own image.	Genesis 1:27	41
J	"The joy of the LORD is your strength."	Nehemiah 8:10	45
K	"Keep my commands and you will live."	Proverbs 4:4	49
L	Your word is a lamp to my feet and a light for my path.	Psalm 119:105	53
M	"For my thoughts are not your thoughts, neither are your ways my ways," declares the LORD.	Isaiah 55:8	57
N	The name of the Lord is a strong tower; the righteous run to it and are safe.	Proverbs 18:10	61
O	"To obey is better than sacrifice."	1 Samuel 15:22	65
P	"For I know the plans I have for you," declares the LORD.	Jeremiah 29:11	69
Q	"He will quiet you with his love."	Zephaniah 3:17	73
R	Remember your Creator in the days of your youth.	Ecclesiastes 12:1	77
S	The Lord is my shepherd, I shall not be in want.	Psalm 23:1	81
T	Give thanks to the LORD, for he is good.	Psalm 136:1	85
U	Trust in the LORD with all your heart and lean not on your own understanding.	Proverbs 3:5	89
V	In the morning, O LORD, you hear my voice.	Psalm 5:3	93
W	"As for God, his way is perfect; the word of the LORD is flawless."	2 Samuel 22:31	97
X	Glorify the LORD with me; let us exalt his name together.	Psalm 34:3	101
Y	You are my hiding place; you will protect me from trouble.	Psalm 32:7	105
Z	It is not good to have zeal without knowledge.	Proverbs 19:2	109

218

26 New Testament Verses

	Memory Verse	Reference	Page
a	And we know that in all things God works for the good of those who love him.	Romans 8:28	113
b	"How beautiful are the feet of those who bring good news!"	Romans 10:15	117
c	"Let the little children come to me."	Matthew 19:14	121
d	"Do to others what you would have them do to you."	Matthew 7:12	125
e	"Everyone who calls on the name of the Lord will be saved."	Romans 10:13	129
f	Forgive as the Lord forgave you.	Colossians 3:13	133
g	"Give, and it will be given to you."	Luke 6:38	137
h	"The Lord is my helper; I will not be afraid."	Hebrews 13:6	141
i	"What is impossible with men is possible with God."	Luke 18:27	145
j	Jesus answered . . . , "You must be born again."	John 3:5–7	149
k	Always try to be kind to each other and to everyone else.	1 Thessalonians 5:15	153
l	"For God so loved the world that he gave his one and only Son, that whoever believes in him shall not perish but have eternal life."	John 3:16	157
m	"Be merciful, just as your Father is merciful."	Luke 6:36	161
n	"'Love your neighbor as yourself.'"	Matthew 19:19	165
o	Children, obey your parents in the Lord.	Ephesians 6:1	169
p	Be patient, bearing with one another in love.	Ephesians 4:2	173
q	Everyone should be quick to listen, slow to speak and slow to become angry.	James 1:19	177
r	Show proper respect to everyone.	1 Peter 2:17	181
s	Seek first his kingdom and his righteousness, and all these things will be given to you.	Matthew 6:33	185
t	"Whoever can be trusted with very little can also be trusted with much."	Luke 16:10	189
u	Do not let any unwholesome talk come out of your mouths, but only what is helpful for building others up.	Ephesians 4:29	193
v	"I am the vine; you are the branches . . . apart from me you can do nothing."	John 15:5	197
w	"'Worship the Lord your God and serve him only.'"	Luke 4:8	201
x	If anything is excellent or praiseworthy—think about such things.	Philippians 4:8	205
y	Don't let anyone look down on you because you are young, but set an example for the believers in speech, in life, in love, in faith and in purity.	1 Timothy 4:12	209
z	"Zacchaeus, come down immediately."	Luke 19:5	213

Scripture Songs

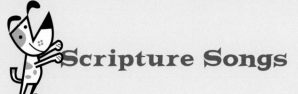

Scripture Songs

Bible Stories

Bible Stories